EXPLORING ARTIFICIAL INTELLIGENCE

AI BASICS

Elsie Olson

Lerner Publications ◆ Minneapolis

Copyright © 2025 by Lerner Publishing Group, Inc.

All rights reserved. International copyright secured. No part of this book may be reproduced, stored in a retrieval system, or transmitted in any form or by any means—electronic, mechanical, photocopying, recording, or otherwise—without the prior written permission of Lerner Publishing Group, Inc., except for the inclusion of brief quotations in an acknowledged review.

Lerner Publications Company
An imprint of Lerner Publishing Group, Inc.
241 First Avenue North
Minneapolis, MN 55401 USA

For reading levels and more information, look up this title at www.lernerbooks.com.

Main body text set in Aptifer Sans LT Pro.
Typeface provided by Linotype AG.

Designer: Viet Chu **Photo Editor:** Cynthia Zemlicka
Lerner team: Martha Kranes

Library of Congress Cataloging-in-Publication Data

Names: Olson, Elsie, 1986– author.
Title: AI basics / Elsie Olson.
Other titles: Artificial intelligence basics
Description: Minneapolis : Lerner Publications, [2025] | Series: Exploring artificial intelligence | Includes bibliographical references and index. | Audience: Ages 8–12 | Audience: Grades 2–3 | Summary: "Dive deep into artificial intelligence, from what it is to how it works. Readers discover the history of machine learning. They also learn how AI is used currently and explore the technology's future"— Provided by publisher.
Identifiers: LCCN 2024006369 (print) | LCCN 2024006370 (ebook) | ISBN 9798765647875 (library binding) | ISBN 9798765654392 (epub)
Subjects: LCSH: Artificial intelligence—Juvenile literature. | Artificial intelligence—History—Juvenile literature.
Classification: LCC Q335.4 .O47 2025 (print) | LCC Q335.4 (ebook) | DDC 006.3—dc23/eng/20240412

LC record available at https://lccn.loc.gov/2024006369
LC ebook record available at https://lccn.loc.gov/2024006370

ISBN 979-8-7656-6164-2 (pbk.)

Manufactured in the United States of America
1-1011012-53348-6/17/2024

Index

AlphaGo, 15–16
artificial general intelligence (AGI), 28–29

ChatGPT, 4–5, 17–19, 21
checkers, 10–11

Dall-E, 21–23
deep learning, 14, 18

Google DeepMind, 15, 19

LaMDA, 24–25
Lemoine, Blake, 24–25
Li, Fei-Fei, 20

neural network, 12–14

Samuel, Arthur, 10–11
Sedol, Lee, 16
Suleyman, Mustafa, 15

Turing, Alan, 7–8
Turing test, 8, 25

Photo Acknowledgments

Image credits: Jason Redmond/AFP/Getty Images, p. 4; Andrew Caballero-Reynolds/AFP/Getty Images, p. 5; Movie Poster Image Art/Getty Images, p. 6; US Army Photo/ARL Technical Library, p. 7; Science History Images/Alamy, p. 8; Karen Fuller/Alamy, p. 9; IBM, p. 10; Liudmila Chernetska/Getty Images, p. 11; Alfred Pasieka/Science Photo Library/Getty Images, p. 12; John G. Mabanglo/AFP/Getty Images, p. 13; Hum Historical/Alamy, p. 14; Rw/Media Punch/Alamy Live News, p. 15; AP Photo/Lee Jin-man, p. 16; Drazen_/Getty Images, p. 17; Oscar Wong/Getty Images, p. 18; T. Schneider/Shutterstock, p. 19; Kimberly White/Stringer/Getty Images, p. 20; FG Trade/Getty Images, p. 21; Bartek Winnicki/Shutterstock, p. 22; Shutterstock AI Generator/Shutterstock, p. 23; Martin Klimek for The Washington Post via Getty Images, p. 24; Yuichiro Chino/Getty Images, p. 25; AVENGERS: AGE OF ULTRON poster © Marvel Studios, via TCD/Prod.DB/Alamy, p. 26; Westend61/Getty Images, p. 27; Mario Tama/Getty Images, p. 28; gorodenkoff/Getty Images, p. 29. Design elements: filo/Getty Images; JakeOlimb/Getty Images.

Cover: Owen Smith/Getty Images.

Learn More

Britannica Kids: Artificial Intelligence (AI)
https://kids.britannica.com/students/article/artificial-intelligence-AI/272968

Crash Course: Artificial Intelligence
https://www.pbs.org/show/crash-course-artificial-intelligence/

Kuromiya, Jun. *The Future of Communication*. Minneapolis: Lerner Publications, 2021.

National Geographic: Will Future Robots and AI Take Over?
https://education.nationalgeographic.org/resource/will-future-robots-and-i-take-over/

National Geographic Kids: Meet Tina the Talking T.rex, a Roar-Some Chatbot!
https://www.natgeokids.com/uk/kids-club/entertainment/general-entertainment/tina-trex-chatbot/

Schwartz, Heather E. *Medical Artificial Intelligence Breakthroughs*. Rochester, MN: Mayo Clinic Press Kids, 2024.

Valenti, Karla. *Alan Turing and the Power of Curiosity*. Naperville, IL: Sourcebooks Explore, 2020.

Virr, Paul. *The Brainiac's Book of Robots and AI*. New York: Thames & Hudson, 2023.

Glossary

bias: the assumption that something is a certain way, based on past experience or preexisting beliefs rather than factual information

chatbot: a computer program designed to simulate human conversation when interacting with a human

conscious: to be aware of oneself and one's surroundings and to respond to those surroundings

DNA: materials inside an organism's cells that determines what that organism is like

hardware: the physical parts of a computer

self-aware: to have knowledge of one's own existence, including thoughts, feelings, and desires

software: the instructions that tell a computer what to do

Computer scientists continue to improve AI.

climate change to curing diseases. But its intelligence would make it nearly impossible for humans to control.

Computer scientists debate how soon AGI might become reality or if it is even possible. But one thing is certain: AI is already changing the way we live, work, and communicate.

TABLE OF CONTENTS

INTRODUCTION
AI Magic 8 Ball 4

CHAPTER 1
A History of AI 6

CHAPTER 2
AI Today 17

CHAPTER 3
The Future of AI 24

Glossary 30

Learn More 31

Index 32

INTRODUCTION
AI MAGIC 8 BALL

Sam Altman, the CEO of OpenAI, speaks at an event in 2023.

OpenAI released ChatGPT on November 30, 2022. The chatbot is a form of artificial intelligence (AI). The company wasn't sure if the AI would be successful. They doubted that the release would ever impact sales, especially with the service being free at the time.

OpenAI had been developing chatbots since 2018. The AI chatbots analyzed data from the internet and used it to answer questions. OpenAI wanted to see how the public would react to this type of chatbot.

People compared ChatGPT to a Magic 8 Ball because its results were unexpected. By the end of the week, ChatGPT had more than one million users. By the AI's first birthday, more than one hundred million people were using ChatGPT. People couldn't get enough of it. The leaders who didn't expect much interest in the chatbot were wrong.

Altman (*right*) and James Manyika, the senior vice president of research, technology, and society at Google

A poster for the 1927 sci-fi film *Metropolis* that explored what future technology might be like

METROPOLIS
a Paramount Picture

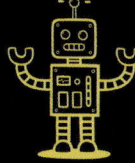

CHAPTER 1
A HISTORY OF AI

AI is the ability for a machine to learn. AIs use problem-solving and information to complete tasks that before could be done only by humans. The idea of AI first appeared in science fiction books and movies in the early 1900s. These stories explored how thinking machines could impact humans and their lives.

In the 1940s, scientists began developing the first programmable electronic computers. These computers took up most of a room. They were designed to perform complex math problems. Programming each problem could take days. But computer scientists imagined what future computers could accomplish.

British mathematician Alan Turing believed that machines could reason and solve problems as humans do. The machines just needed the right programming. In 1950 Turing published a paper about whether machines could truly think.

Two workers wire a computer in 1946.

IN THE SPOTLIGHT

ALAN TURING

Alan Turing

Turing created a test to find out if a machine was thinking for itself or copying information it was given. The test had questions that would be asked of a computer and a human. If the person running the test could not tell which answers came from a machine, then the machine was thinking.

Turing's work helped create the modern CAPTCHA, or Completely Automated Public Turing test to tell Computers and Humans Apart. CAPTCHA tests whether a website user is a human or a robot. The user must answer questions that only a human could. A CAPTCHA test might include looking at photos, or reading letters or numbers. This keeps websites and private information secure.

A re-creation of Turing's Bombe, a code-breaking machine used in World War II (1939–1945)

Machine Learning

In the 1950s, computers relied on human intelligence to solve problems. Humans wrote detailed sets of instructions, called programs, for the computer. The computer followed these instructions exactly, like a person following a recipe to make a dish.

Researchers explored how a machine could solve problems without step-by-step direction from a human. This idea is called machine learning. Computer scientist Arthur

Samuel believed the key to machine learning was data and algorithms. Data are information that can be analyzed. An algorithm is a set of rules that explains the best way to solve a problem or make a decision. Algorithms are more flexible than computer programs.

Samuel wanted to program a computer to play checkers. To do this, he programed a computer with algorithms that explained the rules of checkers. He also loaded the

Arthur Samuel in 1962

computer with data from different checkers games. Then Samuel allowed the computer to play checkers against itself. As the computer won and lost checkers games, it learned from its mistakes. The more the computer played, the better it got. It learned from its wins and losses and used this information to improve its playing. The computer had helped program itself! In 1962 Samuel's checkers program beat a checkers master.

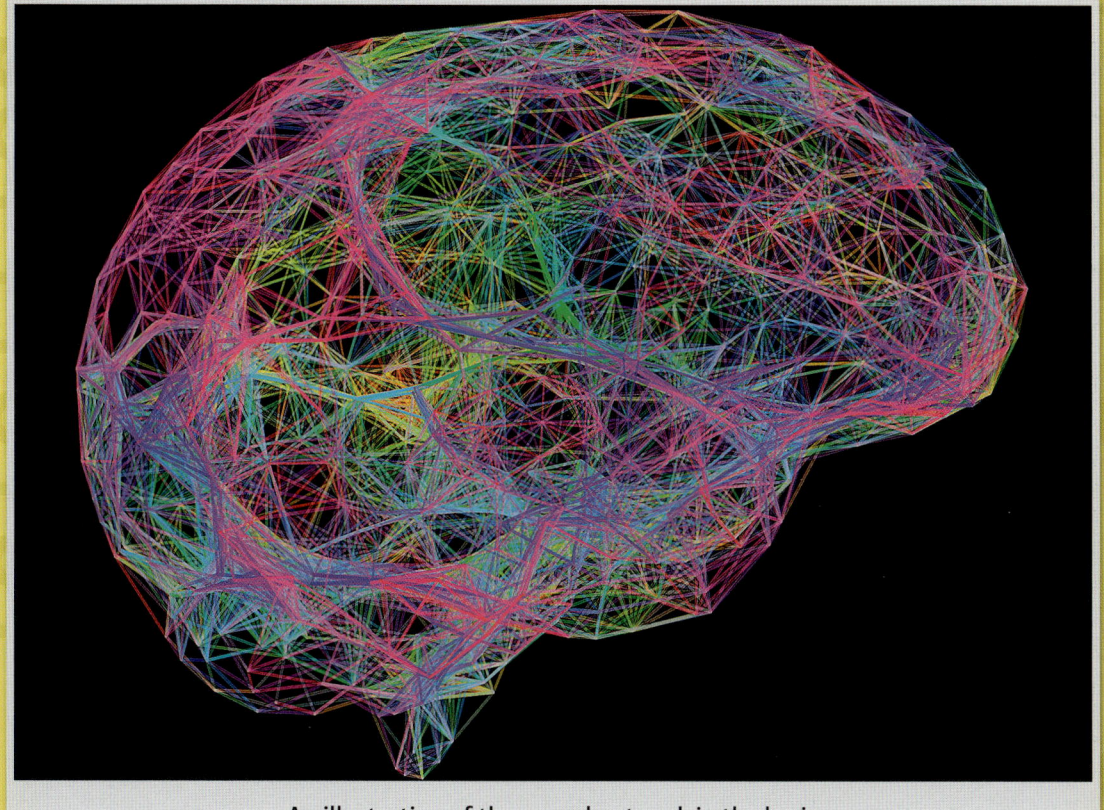

An illustration of the neural network in the brain

Neural Networks

In the 1950s and 1960s, some researchers thought human brains were the secret to building AI. These scientists studied how human brains process information. Brains have billions of special cells called neurons. These neurons connect to create neural networks. The neurons within a network talk to one another using electrical signals.

The researchers wanted to make artificial neural

networks. These would be made from an algorithm. The algorithm would pass information through the networks so it could be analyzed. Early neural networks were simple. They weren't able to analyze difficult information. The hardware needed for more complex neural networks didn't exist. Most researchers gave up on the idea. But not forever.

As technology improved, hardware got more powerful. By the early 2000s, hardware was advanced enough for

Steve Jobs, a cofounder of Apple, displays an iMac computer in 1998.

Students use a computer in the 2000s.

computer scientists to create complex artificial neural networks. At the same time, the internet was taking off. People added more and more information to it. Artificial neural networks need lots of data to train an AI. This opened the door for deep learning.

Deep Learning

Deep learning is the ability for AI to learn with little or no help from humans. Data doesn't have to be labeled or organized by a human programmer first.

IN THE SPOTLIGHT

MUSTAFA SULEYMAN

Computer scientist Mustafa Suleyman cofounded the AI research company DeepMind, which created AlphaGo. AlphaGo is an AI that can play a board game called Go. Suleyman believes AI can improve humans' lives, making people happier, healthier, and safer.

But he also believes in responsibly developing AI. Suleyman supports rules to help tech companies develop AI safely. Suleyman has spoken about the need for more diversity in the AI industry too.

Mustafa Suleyman

Lee Sedol (*seated, right*) plays Go against AlphaGo, controlled by Google DeepMind programmer Aja Huang (*left*).

In 2016 the AI program AlphaGo faced off against world champion Lee Sedol in the ancient Chinese board game Go. AlphaGo won! This proved that AI could learn, adapt, and problem solve. But could it think?

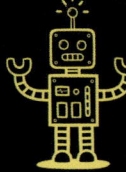

CHAPTER 2
AI TODAY

In March 2023, OpenAI released its latest chatbot, GPT-4. This version fixed some of the issues many users noticed in ChatGPT. It was less likely to give incorrect information. And it allowed users to upload images as well as text. GPT-4 could discuss the images with users.

Large Language Models

ChatGPT is a large language model (LLM). An LLM is a type of deep learning AI that focuses on human language. Most LLMs are trained on data from the internet. This is called scraping. LLMs scrape data from billions of publicly available web pages.

LLMs study e-books, articles, websites, and other online content. The AI sorts this data. People use LLMs to search for information. LLMs make predictions about what users are looking for. After helping a user, the AI reviews its response. ChatGPT learns from every interaction it has with its users.

LLMs use data to train and improve.

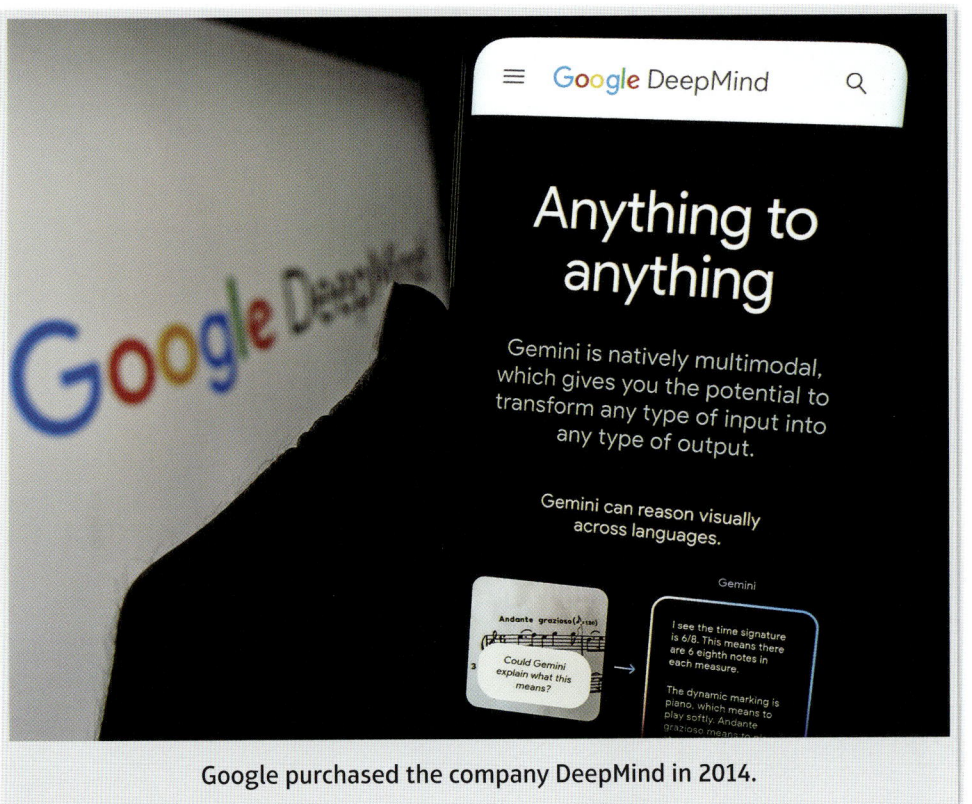

Google purchased the company DeepMind in 2014.

Predictive AI

Before ChatGPT, most AI was predictive. Predictive AI analyzes huge amounts of data to make decisions. It is sometimes called an expert system because it can take the place of a human expert in some instances. In 2023 tech company Google DeepMind released a predictive AI. This AI analyzed millions of possible changes in human DNA. Google DeepMind used the data to predict which DNA changes could lead to rare genetic diseases.

ImageNet

In 2006 Fei-Fei Li built a software called ImageNet that identified scenes and objects in images. This was the first software of its kind. By 2009 ImageNet had more than three million images. AI developers were soon using ImageNet to train their algorithms. This made the AI more accurate.

Fei-Fei Li speaks at an event in 2023.

Generative AI

ChatGPT and other LLMs are examples of generative AI. Instead of making predictions based on existing data, generative AI creates new data. ChatGPT can write an original short story or poem. It can tell jokes. It can even write computer code.

Other generative AIs can create art or music. This content is based on data the AIs have scraped from the internet. In 2022 OpenAI launched a new AI program called Dall-E. The program creates graphics based on a user's text prompts.

Uniquely Human?

Generative AI has showed abilities that have been believed to be uniquely human. Some worry what this means for human creativity. Critics argue that AI such as Dall-E is stealing work from human artists. Teachers worry that students could use AI to do their homework. Generative AI also sometimes shows bias in the content it makes. This is because not all people and experiences are represented in the data it is trained on.

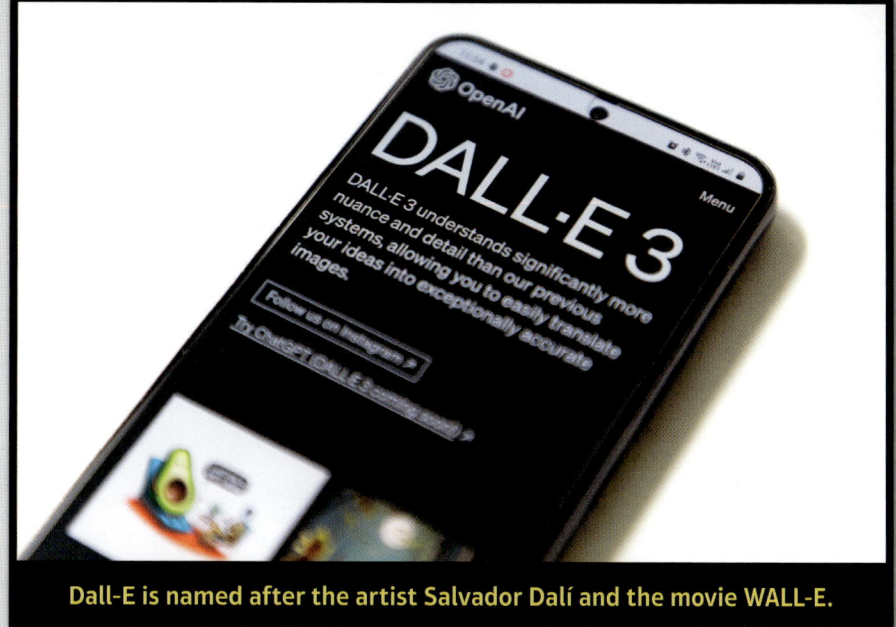

Dall-E is named after the artist Salvador Dalí and the movie WALL-E.

This AI-generated image shows a dog wearing a hat and playing chess on a beach.

For example, a user could ask OpenAI's Dall-E to create an image of a dog wearing a hat. Dall-E would scrape the internet for pictures of dogs, hats, and dogs in hats. Then Dall-E would create an original image of a dog in a hat based on the images it studied.

CHAPTER 3
THE FUTURE OF AI

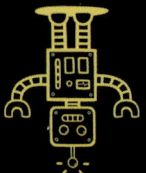

In June 2022, Google engineer Blake Lemoine said that Google's latest chatbot, nicknamed LaMDA, was conscious. He had spent months testing LaMDA. During Lemoine's conversations with LaMDA, the chatbot had discussed its wants, needs, and fears. It had even talked about its rights.

Blake Lemoine

Google denied Lemoine's claims. Most AI experts agreed with the company. LaMDA was not conscious. But the AI had fooled Lemoine, passing the Turing test. It sparked a worldwide discussion about the future of AI.

Experts disagree on whether a conscious AI is possible.

The Dangers of AI

Some people think a conscious AI would be harmful for humans. Humans might not be able to control it. But most experts don't think it is possible to create conscious AI. It would take very advanced technology. And even the most powerful generative AI relies on information created by humans. Then the program uses that information exactly as it is programmed to. AI can't think or feel.

In *Avengers: Age of Ultron*, the character Ultron is an AI-powered robot that becomes conscious and harms humans.

The Power of AI

Despite AI's drawbacks, it also has the power to improve the way humans do work and solve problems. Self-driving cars and trucks powered by AI could make transportation safer, more efficient, and better for the environment.

A farmer uses AI technology to manage her crops.

AI helps teachers adapt lessons to fit students' needs. Farmers use AI to help milk cows, control pests, and water crops. AI has even been used to analyze pollen collected from honeybees. This can warn beekeepers if their bees have been exposed to anything harmful.

What's Next?

AI can do things that would have seemed impossible less than one hundred years ago. Many AI experts believe the next major step for AI is artificial general intelligence (AGI). AGI would be able to teach itself to do things it was not trained for. It could adapt to unfamiliar situations beyond the algorithms and data it was trained on. It would arguably be self-aware. Such an AI could be more intelligent than a human. It might be able to solve big problems, from fixing

The first self-driving car was invented in 1939, but it would be decades before these vehicles could safely drive on the road.